My First Bosnian
Words for Communication

Picture Book with English Translations

Published By: AuthorUnlock.com

živjeli

Cheers

uđite

Come In

čestitam

Congratulations

udes

Crash

opasnost

Danger

izvinite

Excuse Me

požar

Fire

hrana

Food

doviđenja

Goodbye

sretan rođendan

Happy Birthday

zdravo

Hello

upomoć

Help

koliko?

How Many?

lijevo

Left

hajdemo

Let's go

možda

Maybe

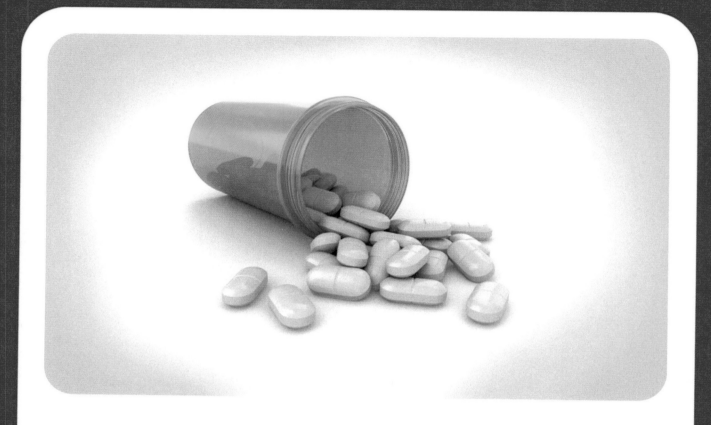

lijek

Medicine

ne

No

ništa

Nothing

molim

Please

vuci

Pull

guraj

Push

desno

Right

izvinjavam

Sorry

uskoro

Soon

uspori

Slow Down

stani

Stop

hvala

Thank You

lopov

Thief

čekaj

Wait

voda

Water

šta?

What?

kada?

When?

gdje?

Where?

ko?

Who?

zašto?

Why?

da

Yes

Made in the USA
Monee, IL
10 August 2020